DRONES ARE EVERYWHERE!

DRONES
FOR FUN

JASON BRAINARD

PowerKiDS press

New York

Published in 2020 by The Rosen Publishing Group, Inc.
29 East 21st Street, New York, NY 10010

First Edition

Editor: Shannon Harts
Book Design: Tanya Dellaccio

Photo Credits: Cover (background) Artazum/Shutterstock.com; cover (drone) Stock image/Shutterstock.com; series background Djem/Shuttertock.com; p. 5 Elena Sherengovskaya/Shutterstock.com; p. 7 Kite_rin/Shutterstock.com; p. 9 VCG/Visual China Group/Getty Images; p. 11 Serbi/Shutterstock.com; p. 13 BorneoJC James/Shutterstock.com; p. 15 Aerial-motion/Shutterstock.com; p. 16 SAKARET/Shutterstock.com; p. 17 Daniel Jedzura/Shutterstock.com; p. 19 Srijaroen/Shutterstock.com; p. 20 KOEN VAN WEEL/AFP/Getty Images; p. 21 Drew Angerer/Getty Images News/Getty Images; p. 22 DZMITRY PALUBIATKA/Shutterstock.com.

Library of Congress Cataloging-in-Publication Data

Names: Brainard, Jason.
Title: Drones for fun / Jason Brainard.
Description: New York : PowerKids Press, 2020. | Series: Drones are everywhere! | Includes glossary and index.
Identifiers: ISBN 9781725309180 (pbk.) | ISBN 9781725309203 (library bound) | ISBN 9781725309197 (6 pack)
Subjects: LCSH: Drone aircraft–Juvenile literature.
Classification: LCC UG1242.D7 B73 2020 | DDC 623.74'69–dc23

Manufactured in the United States of America
CPSIA Compliance Information: Batch #CWPK20. For Further Information contact Rosen Publishing, New York, New York at 1-800-237-9932.

CONTENTS

A NEW KIND OF FUN

It's common to see birds, bugs, and planes flying across the sky. Now there's something new zipping through the air. They look unusual. They sound weird. They move in strange ways. They can hover over your head. What are they? They're drones!

You may have already seen your first drone. While they were once only found in **science fiction** stories, today flying drones is an exciting, or lively and interesting, new hobby that can be fun to master.

DRONE DETAILS

DRONES ARE ALSO KNOWN AS UNMANNED **AERIAL VEHICLES** OR UAVs.

The U.S. government could allow as many as 3.5 million drones by 2021.

WHAT IS A DRONE?

A drone is an aircraft or ship with no human **pilot** on it. Drones are usually flown by a person on the ground. This person uses a **remote control** to direct the drone.

Soldiers used many of the first drones. Companies then began to use drones to spray crops and inspect, or observe, pipes. Soon after that, drones made for fun were ready for **consumers**. Drones were seen as an expensive hobby at first. Today you can buy a drone from many stores and websites.

A drone with four **rotors** is called a quadcopter.

7

PARTS OF A DRONE

Pilots use a remote control to make a drone do what they want it to do. The remote control tells the drone's rotors how fast to spin. This helps a drone change direction.

A small **battery** runs the rotors. A **GPS** unit tells the drone which direction to fly. When the pilot is done flying it, the drone uses landing gears to soften its landing. Many drones also come with a camera for taking pictures.

DRONE DETAILS

DRONE BATTERIES CURRENTLY LAST BETWEEN FIVE AND 30 MINUTES BEFORE THEY NEED TO BE RECHARGED OR **REPLACED**.

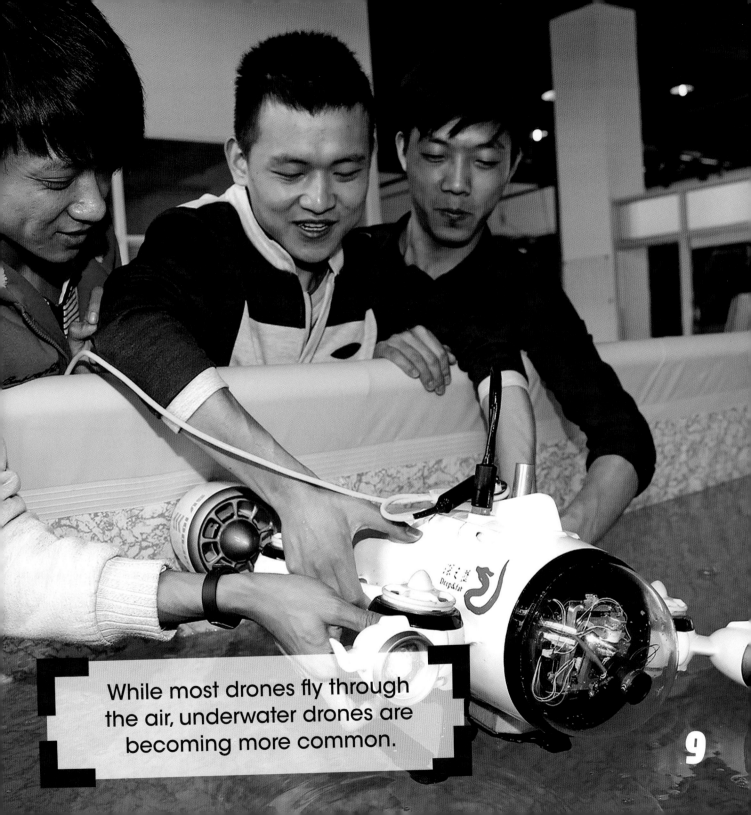

While most drones fly through the air, underwater drones are becoming more common.

YOUR FIRST DRONE

Drones can weigh hundreds of pounds and cost thousands of dollars. A heavy and costly drone is a poor choice for your first drone. Your first drone should be lightweight and inexpensive because you are likely to crash it.

The less expensive it is, the easier it will be to replace. The less it weighs, the less likely you are to hurt yourself or somebody else. Anything falling from the sky can be dangerous, or unsafe. Always remember to be safe when flying your drone.

Drones come in many sizes.
Small and lightweight drones
can also be great for traveling.

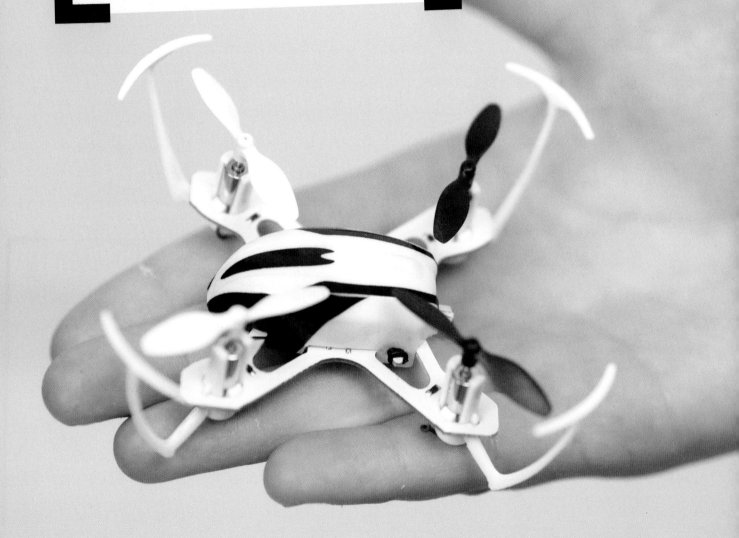

HOW THEY FLY

A rotor on a drone takes air from above and pushes it downward. The air beneath the drone pushes back. This is called lift.

The faster a rotor spins, the more the air beneath the drone pushes back. This sends the drone upward. Once the drone is in the air, your remote control is used to steer, or guide, it. Your remote will tell the drone's computer to spin the rotors at different speeds. This makes your drone move in different directions.

Learning to fly a drone can be tricky. Crashes are common in the beginning.

RULES AND SAFETY TIPS

While flying drones is fun, the Federal Aviation Administration (FAA) has made rules that people must follow to make sure that nobody gets hurt. Never let your drone fly out of sight. If you can't see it, you can't control it.

Don't use your drone to secretly watch others. Would you want someone secretly watching you? Keep your drone flying lower than 400 feet (122 m). Lastly, don't fly your drone near airports or gatherings of people. It could cause someone to suddenly get hurt.

DRONE DETAILS

IT'S ILLEGAL TO FLY A DRONE AT NIGHT, BUT YOU CAN GET SPECIAL PERMISSION TO DO IT AS LONG AS YOU FOLLOW CERTAIN RULES.

Drones allow us to view the world in new and exciting ways.

15

TROUBLESHOOTING

Your drone is powered by a battery. The first thing to do if you have a problem with your drone is check the battery. Make sure that the battery is charged. Some drones use an app on a smartphone as a remote control.

If your drone uses an app, make sure it's up to date. If your drone isn't flying right, check for a bent rotor. You may need to ask an adult for help or search the internet for a fix.

DRONE DETAILS
DRONES AREN'T USUALLY ALLOWED IN U.S. NATIONAL PARKS.

Drones carrying cameras can take beautiful aerial pictures.

HOBBIES OF THE PAST

People have always been drawn to flying. Kites and paper airplanes were made in China centuries ago. Paper airplanes were made before real planes. Flying model rockets was once popular. Have you ever seen an old **balsa** wood glider, or aircraft without an engine? They float through the air.

Watching a **helium**-filled balloon fly up into the sky can be fun, and so is throwing a Frisbee. Drones are simply the latest hobby that lets us pretend to fly. Plus, they can go fast!

Drones can spark creativity and push your imagination in new directions.

19

NOW WHAT?

You may want to show off your new skills once you've learned how to fly your drone. You may want to take it to the next level. But how?

Drone photography and racing are both becoming more popular. Pictures taken by drones can show us the world like we've never seen it before. Drones can take pictures from spots too dangerous for a person. You can have fun racing your friends by joining a drone racing club.

DRONE DETAILS

THE DUTCH POLICE TRIED TRAINING EAGLES TO CATCH DRONES THAT WEREN'T FOLLOWING THE RULES, BUT THEY FOUND THERE WASN'T A GREAT ENOUGH NEED AND IT WAS TOO HARD TO TRAIN THE BIRDS.

Drone racing has brought thousands of people into the world of air sports.

IT'S UP TO YOU

It was once hard to imagine owning and flying a drone. Today you can buy a drone and fly it in your yard or a park. Flying drones as a hobby is so much fun that there likely will soon be millions of them in the United States.

With so many drones in the air, we all must stay safe. Always follow the rules when flying your drone. The fate of drones is in your hands.

DRONE DETAILS

IN 2016, A DRONE DELIVERED PIZZA FOR THE FIRST TIME TO A COUPLE IN NEW ZEALAND.

GLOSSARY

aerial: Occurring in the air.

balsa: A lightweight wood.

battery: A small machine that provides a larger machine with electricity.

consumer: Having to do with people who buy goods and services.

GPS (Global Positioning System): A navigating system that uses satellite signals to tell the user where they are and to direct them to a destination.

helium: A gas that is lighter than air.

pilot: Someone who files an airplane or other flying machine.

remote control: A device that controls a machine from a distance.

replace: To use something instead of something else.

rotor: A rotating blade.

science fiction: Stories about how imagined future scientific events would affect people.

vehicle: A machine that carries goods and people from one place to another.

INDEX

WEBSITES